Happy Birthday

to my favorite father!

You are truly one of the best around, and I love you with all my heart.

Love always, your favorite son

ALSO BY LEO BUSCAGLIA

Love
Seven Stories of Christmas Love
Bus 9 to Paradise
Because I Am Human
The Way of the Bull
The Disabled and Their Parents: A Counseling Challenge
Personhood
The Fall of Freddie the Leaf
Living, Loving, & Learning
Loving Each Other
A Memory for Tino

PAPA, MY FATHER

A CELEBRATION OF DADS

LEO BUSCAGLIA

Library of Congress catalog number: 88-34500
SLACK, Incorporated ISBN: 1-55642-087-0
William Morrow and Company, Inc. ISBN: 0-688-08929-1

Published in the United States of America by:
SLACK, Incorporated
6900 Grove Road
Thorofare, New Jersey 08086

In the United States, distributed to the trade by:
William Morrow and Company, Inc.
105 Madison Avenue
New York, New York 10016

In Canada, distributed to the trade by:
MacMillan of Canada
a Division of Canada Publishing Corporation
164 Commander Boulevard
Agincourt, Ontario
M1S3C7

Library of Congress Cataloging-in-Publication Data

Buscaglia, Leo F.
Papa, my father.

1. Buscaglia, Leo F.—Biography—Family.
2. Buscaglia, Rocco Bartolomeo. 3. Fathers and sons—United States—Biography. 4. Authors, American—20th century—Biography. 5. Italian Americans—California—Social life and customs. I. Title.
PS3552.U8125Z47 1989 813′.54 88-34500
ISBN 0-688-08929-1

Printed in the United States of America

First Edition

1 2 3 4 5 6 7 8 9 10

BOOK DESIGN BY DAVID GATTI

For Rocco Bartolomeo (Tulio) Buscaglia
The man I called Papa, the man
I loved so much . . .
And to all the other fathers
who may never be celebrated,
but who are nonetheless heroes

Acknowledgments

With special thanks to my sisters, Caroline and Margaret, and my Uncle Mario Buscaglia, who helped me to get the facts straight. And to Dan Kimber and Steven Short, who offered ways to better communicate them. Thanks also to Pete Maga for helping me in the search for photos.

No man can possibly know what life means,
what the world means, what anything means,
until he has a child and loves it. And then
the whole universe changes and nothing will
ever again seem exactly as it seemed before.

—LAFCADIO HEARN

Contents

The thing I was always warned against about waiting a long time to have children was that I wouldn't be able to throw a ball with them. Well, I'm here to say that I don't think it's going to be a problem. either I'll throw balls with the best of them and that'll be that, or I won't and it won't matter a damn. Two plus years into this fatherhood business, I know at least that what kids require of their fathers is a lot of attention, a lot of love and, I suspect, if mine ever reach the age of understanding, a lot of that, too. They can find other people to throw balls at them.

—CAREY WINFREY

Certific
Il presente passaporto consta di venti pagine
N. del Passaporto
N. del Registro corrispondente
IN NOME DI SUA MAESTÀ
VITTORIO EMANUELE III
PER GRAZIA DI DIO E PER VOLONTÀ DELLA NAZIONE
RE D'ITALIA
Passaporto
rilasciato a
figlio di
e di
nato a
il
residente a
in provincia di
di condizione

Introduction

It happened when I was supervising an educational program for disabled children many years ago. I was observing in a classroom for mildly retarded fourth graders. I sat beside six children and their teacher in their reading group. They were reading a story about a little duck that had no father. As with all good children's books, this one was filled with repetitive phrases. The refrain was always, "But the little duck had no father."

The teacher, having learned the best technique from her prestigious school of education, read carefully, distinctly, and with feeling. When she completed the story, she followed up immediately with a question-and-answer period to check comprehension, as all good educators do.

"Martha," she asked a lovely little girl in the group, "tell us. Did the little duck have a father?"

The child answered without a moment's hesitation, "Yes."

The teacher paused for a moment, slightly taken aback by the little girl's response. Finally, she smiled and said, "Martha, let me read to you again from the story, and listen very carefully this time."

She then repeated several parts of the story, each time accentuating the familiar refrain, "The little duck had no father."

This time, certain of success, she again asked Martha, "Did the little duck have a father?"

The entire reading group now had fallen into a tense silence while Martha reconsidered the question. After several moments she responded very matter-of-factly, "Yes."

The teacher's frustration was beginning to show at this point, but she was determined that the child would finally get the right answer. With a slight quaver of annoyance revealing itself in her voice, she took the child on her lap, bringing her face close to her own.

"Now listen carefully, Martha. I'm going to read from the story once more." She again read from the book, "The little duck had *no-o-o-o* father." The entire group, and poor Martha, who was now a captive in her teacher's arms, jumped at the sound of the exaggerated "*no!*"

"Now," the teacher asked again sweetly, regaining her control, "did the little duck have a father?"

By this time Martha's large brown eyes had filled with tears of fear and frustration. The entire group waited in anxious silence while she once more thought through the situation carefully. Finally she answered again, "Yes, the little duck had a father."

At this point the teacher totally lost control. "Martha, you disappoint me. You're simply not paying attention! It says again and again in the story that the little duck had *no* father."

Now the tears in Martha's eyes overflowed and ran in streams down her cheeks. "But, teacher," she said, "*everybody* gots a father."

The teacher was taken aback completely. She hugged Martha in apology, smiled, and indicated that now she understood. The entire reading group grinned with relief.

Call him Pa, Da, Dad, Papa, Pater, or what you will, it's all the same—it's universal. "*Everybody* gots a father."

Several decades ago, when I was growing up, it was much easier to define a father. He was the male parent—usually the provider, the ultimate disciplinarian, the decision maker, the symbolic head of the family. When the car stopped working, he fixed it. When a jar stubbornly refused to relinquish its lid, he was summoned to the rescue. If there was a strange noise in the hall, he was the one who investigated it. Most of all, if you had been a brat that day, it was Dad who you were threatened with: "Just wait till your father gets home."

He was gone much of the time at some mysterious place called work, which took him away from home during the day and often occupied his mind at night. It was part of that vast, uncomprehended world of grown-ups that children never fully understand.

At that time it was generally accepted that fathers kept their children at emotional arm's length. The children growing up then looked to their mothers as the nurturers. Dad's job was to "bring home the bacon" and pay the rent. He was the parent about whom a child knew the least. As humorist Erma Bombeck wrote about her father, "When I was a little kid, a father was like a light in the refrigerator. Every house had one, but no one really knew what either of them did once the door was shut."

The media have historically portrayed Dad, when he happened to be present, as a bumbling, ineffectual but lovable person who didn't seem to mind being neglected, ignored, or ridiculed. He was the constant scapegoat for anything horrible, such as "ring around the collar," dandruff on his lapel, or bad breath.

All this was very different from another, earlier image of Father that inspired more fear than respect from his children. He was responsible for putting the "fear of God" into his kids by "not sparing the rod." He was serious, all work and no play, harsh, domineering, and unapproachable.

The last few decades have produced a very altered image of fathers. Their traditional role has changed drastically. It's not uncommon today to find father as nurturer, willing to put urgent matters aside for what he agrees is more important—an active role as family member. He doesn't feel uncomfortable accompanying his children to nursery school, going on class field trips, or proudly watching them perform in the school play, ballet, or baseball game, eagerly recording every action for posterity with his camera.

He is happy to sit patiently while his child performs amazing acts of magic for the fifteenth time, or insists that he solve the riddle just learned from the child next door. He regularly attends backyard parties, dining on mud pies decorated with dandelions and sipping imaginary tea from tin cups.

He is eager to involve himself in honest exchanges of feelings and affection, hoping that he will one day graduate into being one of his child's best friends. He is free of the feeling that he must project an image of infallibility, or that a show of tenderness and vulnerability will threaten his image of masculinity.

He seeks out more active and creative roles in childrearing. He permits himself to respond to his natural instincts, is less reticent to reveal his softer side, eager to show his concern, commitment, and love. He is becoming less driven by work goals—accumulating assets and prestige—and more devoted to the responsibility he has assumed by bringing children into the world.

He is emerging in his new role with the same warmth and concern that, in the past, seemed natural only to mothers.

Not too long ago, at a PTA meeting, I heard a father express his need to be a more active participant in his child's life. "It's a once-in-a-lifetime experience," he said with proud conviction, "and I don't want to miss it. I don't want to discover that my kids and I are strangers to each other. Anyway, why should mothers have all the fun?"

In spite of the none-too-hopeful statistics, a father today has faith that his marriage will be one of the successful ones. He is determined that it will continue to grow and be enhanced by parenthood. His assumption will be correct about half of the time.

The unfortunate ones in the failing 50 percent will have to stand by, often feeling helpless and defeated, as their dreams of a unified, happy family are shattered. They will too often equate the failed relationship with some fault in themselves as human beings—an unnecessarily harsh and self-defeating judgment. They must realize that none of the participants in this very human drama are villains. They are simply people with individual strengths and weaknesses, neither perfect nor faultless. Armed with this basic but essential insight, perhaps they can move from bitterness and blame to the liberation that comes through forgiveness.

There is always hope in the knowledge that adults can learn, change, and grow, and that children are resilient and naturally forgiving. We are too quick to assume that failed marriages leave ruined lives in their wake, without taking into account the human capacity to adapt, to change, and get on with life.

Recently, in a short, informal activity to prepare second graders for the celebration of Father's Day, they were asked to respond to the question "What do you love about your dad?" Their answers were sometimes poignant and often reflective of the fact that nontraditional roles of fatherhood are fast becoming accepted as the norm.

"I love my father, Bob, because we have fun together on weekends, and I love my new father, Al, because he plays with me and fixes me breakfast every morning."

"I love my dad but I don't know where he is. I know he's somewhere because he sends us money all the time, but I don't ever see him."

"I love my dad because he loves me and my brother and my mom and he hugs and kisses us a lot."

"I love my dad because he always brings us things when he visits us on weekends."

I know it has become popular to write books condemning one's parents—about the resentment felt, the irreparable harm they've done, and about their being the underlying cause of some present unhappiness. This is certainly not one of those books. It's also not a book intended to help fathers work through their changing roles. I have neither the inclination nor the expertise it takes to write such a volume.

This book is different. It's a book celebrating the father I grew up with, loved, and with whom I shared so much for so many years. It is a commemoration of the father I knew best—his life, his loves, his actions and what, directly or indirectly, he taught me about life, beauty, and love.

Papa never climbed Everest or made the *Guinness Book of World Records*. He never read the classics or saw an original painting by Braque. He never played baseball and rarely won at bocce ball. He was born poor and, in spite of his working hard all his life, he was always poor. He was proud, self-taught, and left no debts. If he had any hidden dreams, other than of being a good man, a committed father, and a loving husband, no one ever knew about them. If deep regrets, fears, or personal doubts tormented him, he never stated them.

I am aware that years of having known and loved my father have transformed him from Papa, the simple human being, into Papa, the near saint. And I've come to the conclusion that there is nothing wrong with that. Creating saints of our departed loved ones can help us to fill the void and make the parting easier.

But there are still so many things that Papa's death left unresolved—things that haunt, frustrate, and mystify me. There are so many questions I feel that I should have asked my father and never did. Were there right questions to ask? Was I too occupied or embarrassed to deal with them? Was I concerned only with those questions that pertained to me?

It is rather frightening, then, that though I was so close to Papa for so long and loved him so much, I may be presenting only a series of reminiscences of him, perhaps enhanced or distorted by my memory, rather than revealing the truly wonderful, complicated man he was. Perhaps the best I can do is try.

It makes me question whether we can ever really know other people, or if, no matter how close we are to them or how many years we love them, they remain a mystery. Perhaps this insight and the possibilities it suggests to all of us are Papa's ultimate gift.

PAPA,

the Husband

IVREA
AOSTA

There are two sorts of heartwarming domestic comedies on American television. One deals with the daily doings of the young husband and the young wife, who converse for thirty minutes without exchanging a civil word. The other features Father, showing him, to quote a recent writer, as "a miserable chinless halfwit with barely enough mechanical skill to tie his own shoes." Almost any domestic crisis will do to make him a mockery and a scorn to twenty million viewers.

—P. G. WODEHOUSE

I don't believe that Papa, as most men, ever thought much about being a husband or father. He got married and, therefore, became a husband. He had a child and so became a father. It was as natural and as simple as that. When he died at age eighty-eight, I don't for a moment think that he felt either role had required any great sacrifice. When I wrote my first book, *Love*, I dedicated it to my parents who, I wrote, "never taught me about love—they showed me." I went on to explain that they were (though I was unaware of it at the time) my models for an understanding of the day-to-day dynamics of love.

From all outward appearances, one could not imagine a less despotic husband than Papa. He never seemed to demand anything. He took things pretty much as they came. He had an uncanny way of telling us what he was feeling—more with his eyes than with his words. In his eyes was that look that congratulated Mama for a good meal or alerted us that there would be hell to pay for our disruptive behavior. And it was a look that told us, at very special moments, how proud he was to be our father.

I can't recall too many unhappy moments or angry arguments between my parents, though these things certainly occurred. When they happened, it was usually Papa who flew into rages, threats, and table poundings. When he lost his temper, a deep red flush came over his face and his lips would form into a scowl. It was astounding how quickly he could switch from warm and docile to raging and tyrannical. At these times Mama would attempt to be rational and defend herself with logical arguments, but when Papa was going full tilt, he was not terribly receptive to logic. He was more interested in release. Mama's ultimate defense was tears. They always worked their magic. It was impossible for Papa to resist Mama's tears. Her eyes, so soft and transparent, would fill and the argument was over.

Mama and Papa never tried to conceal their anger or hide an argument from their children. Their differences were always solved on the spot, no matter how uncomfortable it was for those present. I don't remember their disagreements ever ending in bitterness or vindictiveness. Once expressed, the angry feelings seemed to disappear as quickly as they had appeared. Any remaining differences soon gave way to a show of affection.

All this helped me to learn early in life that parents are people, too; that neither is perfect and that conflict arises even among those who love each other. I am certain that learning this as a child saved me from a great deal of anguish later.

Mama was more relaxed than Papa. He required order in his daily life. He was always strikingly neat in appearance, always put his soiled clothes in the laundry hamper, and hung up his jackets in the closet, forever putting things back where he got them. He was neurotic about waste and insisted that we turn off the lights when we left a room, or closed doors behind us to keep the heat in. He had a special fetish about shutting the refrigerator door. He assured us he wasn't working so hard all day to support the electric company. Breaking any of these house rules was a serious offense, seldom repeated twice.

But most of the time Papa was a soft touch. He was never fearful of revealing his vulnerability. We often saw him cry. One such occasion stands out and is centered (as most of my most vivid memories are) around the dinner table, a place where problems were shared, discussed, and often solved. Papa announced that a business partner and friend had absconded with all their financial resources and left him bankrupt! He wept with disappointment and feelings of betrayal. We all sat silent until he had wiped his tears. He looked at us silently for a while and then asked, "What shall we do now?"

Papa's problems, as well as his tears, were a part of all of us. I don't think I ever loved my father as much as I did at that moment. After all, we were a family, and Papa was in trouble. He was sharing his adult pain with me, a child. He was receptive to my feelings and *my* input. He had asked, "What are *we* going to do?"

Of course, Mama was the first to come to the rescue. "Never mind," was her usual reply at such times, "it's not the end of the world." She reassured Papa that we had a garden full of things to eat and we were all healthy and alive. She was convinced that God would find a way, reminding us all that with God on our side we could never fail.

Her solutions were simple. Mama would sell eggs and take in washing as she used to. My elder brother and sister would quit school for a while and go to work. My other sister would help Mama with the house and chores. I would get a job selling magazines door to door—*The Saturday Evening Post* always needed boys.

We all agreed that it wasn't only Papa's responsibility to feed and clothe the family. We also had an obligation to one another. His tears convinced me again that Papa was different from other fathers I saw. I was glad that he was.

Papa loved to make Mama happy, and one way guaranteed to do so was to take her on an excursion. She especially loved going to Long Beach, about thirty miles away from our home in east Los Angeles. At that time, without freeways, it was no small thing. But our trips were *always* a major project for Papa. Mama wouldn't travel unless she could do so in comfort. She wanted first class all the way, Mama's notion of first class being quite different from most other people's.

Papa began preparations days prior to the trip. It required getting out the beach chairs, the umbrella and its stand, and the matching protective curtain. He had to pack the grill, a turpentine stove, pots and pans, dishes, eating utensils, and swim wear for the entire family (and friends). It was understood that there were to be no shortcuts for Mama's outing; regular meals of four or five courses were to be cooked at the beach. We had only a two-door car at the time and with six or eight people to transport, along with all the necessary paraphernalia for Mama's pleasure, it was no mean job to get things ready for the journey. There was not a square inch of unused space in that old car when we hit the road.

But Papa would go a long way to make his Rosina smile. We started at dawn, early enough to get the choice place on the sand (Mama's choice, that is). We were always first to arrive, our car looking as if we'd come across the country rather than across town. We were always last to leave. "People are strange," Mama would say. "Just when the beach is the most beautiful, at dusk, everybody leaves it to the seagulls." Of course, she was right, as usual.

The loading and unloading of the car was a traumatic time for everyone but Mama. She stood by and directed the project like a factory foreman—umbrella here, chairs there, cooking equipment downwind, food in the shade, icebox under the umbrella. It seemed hours before everything was in place and we were allowed to change into bathing suits and make a run for the water. By then, Papa's patience was growing thin.

No sooner were we settled than it was time for him

to fire up the stove and make preparations for the elaborate lunch Mama had carefully planned. Now the beach was crowded with glistening bodies baking in the summer sun. Those who were near us were quite obviously fascinated by our complicated beach arrangements. We were giving them a show that surely would keep them talking for weeks.

When lunch was over, Mama would hike up her skirts and bathe her feet in the cool ocean. Then it was time for a nap in the shade of the umbrella, behind the curtain drawn around us. Mama always insisted that we remove our wet swimsuits before we napped. She would construct a small clothesline to dry everything in the sea breezes. Then, body to body, we went to sleep.

In reality, the nap was just a respite between meals. We all knew that there was another feast to come. Though Papa growled that he was married to a crazy lady and this would be the last time we'd ever come to the beach, he secretly enjoyed the whole ritual. As the day wore on and he saw the joy that his labors created, he finally joined in the madness, relaxed, and enjoyed it.

When dinner was over, we were usually the last remaining humans on the beach. This was a signal to do everything in reverse, as we got things repacked and loaded for our return trip. It always seemed a tighter squeeze going home, our stomachs as filled to capacity as the car was. The long voyage home was always preceded by a short visit to the boardwalk—looking at the lights, listening to the roar of the cyclone racer and the laughter from the fun house, and the screams from people smashing into each other in the bumper cars. We were seldom allowed to go on the rides because Papa could think of a thousand better ways to spend money, but it was fun to watch from the sidelines, too.

The sun had gone down and the cool of the evening was perfect for our ride home. Though we were all exhausted, we were much too wound up to sleep. This part of our voyage became a song. We may not have sung well, but we did sing with enthusiasm and passion. "Mairzy Doats," "Donkey Serenade," "Giannina Mia" and the top-ten tunes of the Hit Parade were all sung in our unique family harmony. What may have been lacking in quality was more than made up for in volume.

The trip didn't seem long. My brother was always at the wheel, someone was in Mama's lap, and someone in Papa's. The rest of us were squeezed together like chickens on the way to market. Sleep was never a problem when we returned home after one of Mama's outings.

Far more adventuresome were our trips to San Diego. We would take off before dawn, settling in for the three- or four-hour ride. The roads were different in those days, of course, and there was one dreaded obstacle to our trip that almost always brought us to a grinding halt—the terrible Torrey Pines grade, about forty miles north of San Diego. With our trusty Chevy loaded beyond capacity, as usual, we would all say a tense, silent prayer as the engine strained to pull us over the hill. With the radiator at boiling point and steam rising ominously from the hood, my brother would pull off the road with a sigh, "Well, that's it for this trip."

This announcement might have been cause for despair for other travelers, but it was never so with us. Aware that we would never arrive at our intended destination, Papa would proceed to unload the car for lunch. If we could not eat in lovely Balboa Park in San Diego, at least we would do so in the shade of the twisted Torrey Pines. "Never mind," Papa would say, "we won't have as long a drive home."

Papa loved to take evening walks with Mama. There was a great mystery about these walks, and though we would plead to go with them, it was always "no kids allowed." We wondered where they went and what they did when they got there. We certainly could not imagine that they had no destination. What could they possibly still have to talk about after so many years? We stayed behind to wash dishes, clean off the kitchen table, take out the trash, and wait for their return. The mysterious walks never took less than an hour.

Mama was always proud of her husband and well she

should have been. He was intelligent, handsome, sensitive, caring, and attentive. During all the years I saw them together, I can't recall Mama ever looking full face at Papa. In fact, we were told that she never actually took a good look at Papa until their wedding night, theirs having been a mostly arranged marriage and Mama being very shy. She never got over her shyness when it came to Papa. I'm certain, though, she had ample opportunity to admire him with side glances until the day she died, after sixty-one years together.

Perhaps Papa wasn't the perfect husband, but it seems to me that he came close. One thing is certain: Mama never asked for anything more.

PAPA,

the Educator

THE EXPANSION OF THE UNITED STATES 215
many federal offices. Having thus swept away everything
that seemed "monarchical" and "un-American," the Re-
publicans sought to encourage agriculture, which they
Land for the Farmers.

When I was a boy of fourteen, my father was so ignorant I could hardly stand to have the old man around. But when I got to be twenty-one, I was astounded at how much he had learned in seven years.

—MARK TWAIN

Papa had natural wisdom. He wasn't educated in the formal sense. When he was growing up at the turn of the century in a very small village in rural northern Italy, education was for the rich. Papa was the son of a dirt-poor farmer. He used to tell us that he never remembered a single day of his life when he wasn't working. The concept of doing nothing was never a part of his life. In fact, he couldn't fathom it. How could one do nothing?

He was taken from school when he was in the fifth grade, over the protestations of his teacher and the village priest, both of whom saw him as a young person with great potential for formal learning. Papa went to work in a factory in a nearby village, the very same village where, years later, he met Mama.

For Papa, the world became his school. He was interested in everything. He read all the books, magazines, and newspapers he could lay his hands on. He loved to gather with people and listen to the town elders and learn about "the world beyond" this tiny, insular region that was home to generations of Buscaglias before him. Papa's great respect for learning and his sense of wonder about the outside world were carried across the sea with him and later passed on to his family. He was determined that none of his children would be denied an education if he could help it.

Papa believed that the greatest sin of which we were capable was to go to bed at night as ignorant as we had been when we awakened that day. This credo was repeated so often that none of us could fail to be affected by it. "There is so much to learn," he'd remind us. "Though we're born stupid, only the stupid remain that way." To ensure that none of his children ever fell into the trap of complacency, he insisted that we learn at least one new thing each day. He felt that there could be no fact too insignificant, that each bit of learning made us more of a person and insured us against boredom and stagnation.

So Papa devised a ritual. Since dinnertime was family time and everyone came to dinner unless they were dying of malaria, it seemed the perfect forum for sharing what new things we had learned that day. Of course, as children we thought this was perfectly crazy. There was no doubt, when we compared such paternal concerns with other children's fathers, Papa was weird.

It would never have occurred to us to deny Papa a request. So when my brother and sisters and I congregated in the bathroom to clean up for dinner, the inevitable question was, "What did *you* learn today?" If the answer was "Nothing," we didn't dare sit at the table without first finding a fact in our much-used encyclopedia. "The population of Nepal is. . . ," etc.

Now, thoroughly clean and armed with our fact for the day, we were ready for dinner. I can still see the table piled high with mountains of food. So large were the mounds of pasta that as a boy I was often unable to see my sister sitting across from me. (The pungent aro mas were such that, over a half century later, even in memory they cause me to salivate.)

Dinner was a noisy time of clattering dishes and endless activity. It was also a time to review the activities of the day. Our animated conversations were always conducted in Piedmontese dialect since Mama didn't speak English. The events we recounted, no matter how insignificant, were never taken lightly. Mama and Papa always listened carefully and were ready with some comment, often profound and analytical, always right to the point.

"That was the smart thing to do." "*Stupido,* how could you be so dumb?" "*Così sia,* you deserved it." "*E allora*, no one is perfect." "*Testa dura* ('hardhead'), you should have known better. Didn't we teach you anything?" "Oh, that's nice." One dialogue ended and immediately another began. Silent moments were rare at our table.

Then came the grand finale to every meal, the moment we dreaded most—the time to share the day's new learning. The mental imprint of those sessions still runs before me like a familiar film clip, vital and vivid.

Papa, at the head of the table, would push his chair back slightly, a gesture that signified the end of the eating and suggested that there would be a new activity. He would pour a small glass of red wine, light up a thin, potent Italian cigar, inhale deeply, exhale, then take stock of his family.

For some reason this always had a slightly unsettling effect on us as we stared back at Papa, waiting for him to say something. Every so often he would explain why he did this. He told us that if he didn't take time to look at us, we would soon be grown and he would have missed us. So he'd stare at us, one after the other.

Finally, his attention would settle upon one of us. "*Felice*," he would say to me, "tell me what you learned today."

"I learned that the population of Nepal is . . ."

Silence.

It always amazed me, and reinforced my belief that Papa was a little crazy, that nothing I ever said was considered too trivial for him. First, he'd think about what was said as if the salvation of the world depended upon it.

"The population of Nepal. Hmmm. Well."

He would then look down the table at Mama, who would be ritualistically fixing her favorite fruit in a bit of leftover wine. "Mama, did you know that?"

Mama's responses were always astonishing and seemed to lighten the otherwise reverential atmosphere. "Nepal," she'd say. "Nepal? Not only don't I know the population of Nepal, I don't know where in God's world it is!" Of course, this was only playing into Papa's hands.

"*Felice*," he'd say. "Get the atlas so we can show Mama where Nepal is." And the search began. The whole family went on a search for Nepal. This same experience was repeated until each family member had a turn. No dinner at our house ever ended without our having been enlightened by at least a half dozen such facts.

As children, we thought very little about these educational wonders and even less about how we were being enriched. We couldn't have cared less. We were too impatient to have dinner end so we could join our less-educated friends in a rip-roaring game of kick the can.

In retrospect, after years of studying how people learn, I realize what a dynamic educational technique Papa was offering us, reinforcing the value of continual learning. Without being aware of it, our family was growing together, sharing experiences, and participating in one another's education. Papa was, without knowing it, giving us an education in the most real sense.

By looking at us, listening to us, hearing us, respecting our opinions, affirming our value, giving us a sense of dignity, he was unquestionably our most influential teacher.

I decided upon a career in teaching fairly early in my college years. During my training, I studied with some of the most renowned educators in the country. When I finally emerged from academia, having been generously endowed with theory and jargon and technique, I discovered, to my great amusement, that the professional educators were imparting what Papa had known all along. He knew there was no greater wonder than the human capacity to learn, that no particle of knowledge was too insignificant not to have the power to change us for the better. "How long we live is limited," Papa said, "but how much we learn is not. What we learn is what we are. No one should miss out on an education."

Papa was a successful educator. His technique worked and has served me well all my life. Now, when I get home, often exhausted after a long working day's adventure, before my head hits the pillow I hear Papa's voice resound clearly in my room. "*Felice*," he asks, "what did you learn today?"

On some days I can't recall even one new thing I have learned. I'm surprised at how often this is the case (since most of us move in a world of the familiar and are too preoccupied to be bothered or challenged by the unfamiliar). I get myself out of bed and scan the bookshelves to find something new. Then, with that accomplished, Papa and I can rest soundly, assured that a day has not been wasted. After all, one never can tell when knowing the population of Nepal may prove to be a very useful bit of information.

PAPA,

the Philanthropist

The quality of a child's relationship with his or her father seems to be the most important influence in deciding how that person will react to the world.

—JOHN NICHOLSON

People were always drawn to Papa—men, women, children—even animals. The one thing that he didn't attract was money. He was one of those individuals who, in spite of his intelligence and ambition, worked hard all his life without ever achieving financial success. He started working as a child and, except for a few brief holidays now and again, never stopped working until he was in his late sixties.

He had jobs in noisy factories, greasy kitchens, crowded hotels, and frenzied restaurants. Though he was a consistently valued employee, he was always somehow passed over at promotion time. Twice he started his own businesses and both times they were successes. But both times the partners whom he trusted found means of easing him out or absconding with the profits, leaving him with accumulated debts.

Papa was forever considered too generous. It was a common thing to hear people say of him, "He's too good. He's not aggressive enough. He's too meek, and in America the meek don't inherit much of anything, let alone the earth."

I remember some difficult times when I was growing up, times when we questioned whether we'd have enough food to eat or be able to meet the monthly bills. But I never recall having been hungry, and never at any time did it occur to me that Papa might be a failure.

For Papa, giving was a way of life. He loved to give.

The things that he owned never seemed to weigh him down the way they do most people. In fact, friends had to be careful not to express a desire for something that was his to give—the tie around his neck or the picture on his wall—or he would surely find a way to give it to them.

Papa didn't understand money. He was never sure what to do with it, especially how to use it as a tool for making more. To him the greatest gifts had nothing to do with money. He gave of himself—his love, his time. He was always ready with a listening ear, an encouraging hug, a well-timed visit, a glass of his homemade wine and whatever he had reaped of the plentiful harvest from his garden: fruit, flowers, vegetables, including the ubiquitous zucchini.

Anyone who has ever tried a hand at gardening knows that there is no more rewarding plant than the zucchini. It takes little care, looks beautiful, and even produces an edible bloom that, when fried in butter, is food for the gods. In addition, its yield is endless.

Papa harvested his zucchini very early, when the squash were small, thin, and tender. That was when he felt they were most flavorful. The quality was surpassed only by their quantity, for no matter how many he picked, there were always more. Thanks to this bounty, Papa gathered enough zucchini to feed a small nation; he'd clean them, separate them by size, and get ready for his rounds.

The most tender of the crop were designated as the ones to be given away. Those that had managed to hide under the bushes and had grown to gargantuan size were for our table. But we were not to be pitied: Over the years Mama had learned how to plan for the bumper crop. She would fry them, steam them, mash them, and stuff them. The possibilities were endless. When we got to the point when one more bite of zucchini might turn us into one, she'd disguise them in casseroles and mix them with fruit and nuts, grate them into a frittata with eggs and garlic, julienne them into an antipasto, or throw them into the minestrone pot. Nothing in our house ever went to waste, but the biggest challenge was the zucchini. It was the kind of challenge Mama was always ready for.

Papa had a regular zucchini route. He portioned off the precious vegetable according to the needs of our neighbors—their family size and gourmet tastes. Six for this family, five for this, and nine for this, until the entire neighborhood was supplied.

Though Papa loved sharing the fruits of his labors, it was not always appreciated. Especially was this true of the young kids in the neighborhood who hated vegetables and for whom zucchini was the most distasteful. As my father visited each house in turn, disappearing through the front door with his bounty in hand, the kids would surround me and threaten me with violence if my father didn't stop giving their parents those "awful green things."

They assured me that if I didn't do something to curb his generosity I'd surely be sorry. I knew this wasn't an idle threat, either. Tony, Chester, and Teddy were all twice my size. Never did I feel so vulnerable, caught between Papa's generosity and the wrath of the kids on the block.

"Please, Papa," I'd plead, "don't take zucchini to the neighbors."

"Why not?"

"Because they hate them." I tried to explain.

"You crazy? Nobody hates zucchini." He dismissed the idea.

Papa's giving wasn't limited to vegetables. He was a soft touch for every beggar in town. "It could be me, you know," he'd say, dropping a few precious coins into a hat.

He always had a cold drink ready for the mail carrier or meter reader. "He's out all day in the hot sun. His job isn't easy."

He was ready with a bunch of flowers for Mrs. Z., confined to her bed with an illness. "She's all alone. She needs pretty things around. It'll make her feel better. Maybe she'll visit me someday when I'm sick."

He would prepare a bottle of wine for the visiting teacher, much to our horror and embarrassment. "It'll help her when she has to read all those papers."

There was ravioli for the librarian. "She gives us all those books free. We can give her a few ravioli. They'll be good for her. She's too skinny, anyway."

I must admit that at the time Papa's giving was a source of great embarrassment to me. No other father in the neighborhood went door to door with zucchini, or gave wine to the teacher. Why couldn't my papa be like other fathers and just not be so visible? Why did he have to be so prominent in the neighborhood?

But as I matured I began to notice a very interesting phenomenon. It was only Papa whose mail was delivered hand to hand. It was only Papa who was warmly greeted by everyone from the trash collector to the local butcher. It was always Papa who got first choice of the new Italian books at the library. I don't think I ever heard anyone speak ill of Papa. Statements about his softness, meekness, and excessive goodness were heard, in time, more like compliments than criticism.

Philanthropy is often equated with money or wealth. Still, the dictionary definition of the word is simply "one who shows goodwill toward all, whose actions and efforts are directed toward promoting human welfare." The word has its roots in the Greek language, meaning "love for mankind." If this is so, then Papa was certainly among the world's greatest, albeit poorest, philanthropists.

PAPA,

the Philosopher

His heritage to his children wasn't words or possessions, but an unspoken treasure, the treasure of his example as a man and a father. More than anything I have, I'm trying to pass that on to my children.

—WILL ROGERS, JR.

It's not easy being different, especially as a child. The normal process of growing up presents enough problems, but when we discover that we deviate from the norm in some way, the problems can only intensify.

There can be no doubt that my family was different. My parents spoke little English, and when they did, it was thick with Italian flavor. Our life-style was obviously unlike most others—a little bit of Mediterrania transferred to the shores of America. We ate different, exotic foods; our conversations were more animated; our voices a bit louder; our gestures more generous. The world we lived in was decidedly more foreign.

As a young child I was neither aware nor concerned about our many differences. Children are naturally more accepting of things as they are, less apt to notice, let alone judge, differences in people unless influenced by adults. But this changed as I grew to adolescence and entered junior high school.

At that time Papa and Mama, whom I had loved without question, suddenly became an embarrassment. Why couldn't they be like other parents? Why didn't they speak without the telltale accents? Why couldn't I have cornflakes for breakfast instead of hard rolls and *caffe latte*? Why couldn't I take peanut butter and jelly sandwiches in my school lunches rather than calamari? ("Yuck," the other kids would say, "Buscaglia eats octopus legs!") There simply seemed no way for me to escape the painful stigma I felt in being Italian and the son of Tulio and Rosa. Buscaglia—even my name became a source of distress.

It was common in those days to label Italians wops and dagos. (Look at him and watch a day go by!) I was never really certain what either of those terms meant, but I nevertheless felt their sting. This pain was acutely felt one day as I prepared to leave school. I found myself unexpectedly surrounded by a group of boys shouting the familiar epithets.

One of them threw a cake at me, the sugary icing splashing across my face, into my hair, and over my clothing. "Dirty dago!" they shouted. "Your dad's a Chicago gangster and your mom's a garlic licker and you're a son of a dirty wop. Why don't you all pack up and go back where you came from?"

It seemed an eternity before I was released from their circle of pushes and punches. Humiliated and in tears, I broke free and dashed home. As I ran, full of confusion, anger, and resentment, I realized I had not made a single attempt to fight back.

When I arrived home, I immediately headed for and locked myself in the bathroom, assuring that I would not be seen. I couldn't stand the prospect of Mama or Papa finding me in my distraught condition. I washed off the frosting that stuck to me like glue. I couldn't stop crying as tears mixed with my blood-smeared face. The frustration enraged and strangled me. I couldn't believe what had happened. It all seemed so very wrong, yet I felt helpless to do anything about it.

It was Papa who finally knocked on the bathroom door. "What are you doing in there? What's the matter?" he questioned. Only after much gentle persuasion did I finally unlatch the door and let him in.

"What happened?" he asked, taking me into his arms. "What's the matter? What is it?"

In his protective arms I allowed myself the release I sorely needed. I sobbed uncontrollably. He sat on the edge of the bathtub with me and waited for me to gain some control. A shattered ego takes much longer to heal than a bloody nose. "Now tell me what happened," he said.

I explained.

When I finished the story, I waited. I expected Papa to make some healing comment or take some immediate defensive action that would soothe me and solve the problem. I envisioned his taking off in search of the bullies who had hurt me, or at least finding their parents and demanding retribution. But Papa didn't move.

"I see," he said quietly. "It's finally happened. They finally found you. Those people who hurt us and make us cry. They don't know us, but they hate us all the same. Those cowards who are strong only in groups and pick on us because they know we're few and not likely to fight back. I know they hurt you, but what happened wasn't meant just for you. You just happened to come along. It could have been any one of us."

"I hate being Italian!" I confessed angrily. "I wish I could be *anything* else!"

Papa held me firmly, his voice now strong and threatening. "Never let me hear you say that again!" he said. "You should be proud to be what you are. Just think about it. America was discovered by and got its name from Italians. Italians make sweet music, sing gloriously, paint wonderful pictures, write great books, and build beautiful buildings. How can you not be proud to be an Italian? And you're extra lucky because you're an American, too."

"But they don't know that," I objected. "I'd rather be like everyone else."

"Well, you're not like everyone else. God never intended us all to be the same. He made us all different so that we'd each be ourselves. Never be afraid of differences. Difference is good. Would you want to be like the boys who beat you up and called you names? Would you want to make others suffer and cry? Aren't you glad you're different from them?" I remember that I thought it was a weak argument, but I remained silent.

"Well, would you?" he insisted. "Would you want to be like them? Like the people who hurt you?"

"No."

"Then wipe your tears and be proud of who you are. You can be sure it won't be the last time you'll meet these people. They're everywhere. Feel sorry for them, but don't be afraid of them. We've got to be strong and always be proud of who we are and what we are. Then nobody can hurt us."

He dried my tears and washed my face. "Now," he said, "let's get some bread and butter and go eat in the garden."

Though I didn't find Papa's explanation very satisfying, it somehow made me feel better. Perhaps it was just that being heard, loved, and held made it seem enough. I was still frustrated about people who had the capacity to be so cruel, who persisted in using others as scapegoats for their own inadequacies, and letting them get away with it.

Further experience has taught me that I was not alone, that these painful encounters—even worse—had happened to my Jewish friends, my Mexican friends, my black friends, my Catholic friends, my Protestant friends, my disabled friends.

Papa was right in teaching me that as long as there was ignorance there would be injustice, as long as there were those with unrecognized self-hate there would be persecution. It is an unfortunate fact of life that the scapegoats are almost always members of a minority group.

Still, Papa made loving the unlovable his greatest challenge. "Bring them home with you, *Felice*," he'd say. "When they know us, they won't be able to hate us anymore."

Of course, Papa didn't solve the problems of bigotry

on that sunny California day when we ate bread and butter in the garden. But there was something in his explanation, a certain strength and determination, that has continued to help me to see intolerance and discrimination for what they are: a refuge for weakness and ignorance. Acceptance and understanding can be expected only from the strong.

PAPA,

the Oenophile

I realize how apt a symbol wine is of life, for it represents sap, vigor, vitality and continuity.

—JEAN-PAUL KAUFFMANN

Like all good Italians, Papa loved his wine, although I never knew him to drink to excess. A glass or two of wine to accompany his dinner was his limit. He never touched hard liquor.

Papa's love of wine went far beyond the simple enjoyment of drinking it. He was truly an oenophile, a connoisseur. He always made his own wine, from ripened grapes to dated label. His cool, dark cellar was full of dusty bottles and cylindrical, wooden barrels of varying sizes, all carefully marked to indicate the type of grape and the year of the harvest.

When I was growing up, we had many festivities in our home. None, except Christmas and Easter, topped the one night each year that we made the new wine. The anticipation and preparation began in July and August, long before the eventful September evening when the truckload of grapes was delivered. By then Papa had made several visits to his friends—grape growers in Cucamonga, about forty miles from our home—to observe the progress of his grapes. He had spent hours scouring the barrels in which the wine would be made and stored, and applying antirust varnish on every visible metal part of the wine-making equipment. The fermenting vat had been filled with water to swell the wood.

On the appointed evening, the truck would arrive after nightfall, brimming with small, tough-skinned, sweet-smelling Cabernet grapes. The boxes of grapes were hand-carried about two hundred feet to the garage, where a giant empty vat awaited. A hand-powered crusher was positioned precariously on top of the vat, ready to grind noisily into the night, as thousands of grapes were poured into it. It was an all-male operation that included Papa, his relatives, and friends. Dressed in their undershirts, bodies glistening with perspiration, they took turns cranking the crusher handle. My job was to stack the empty crates neatly out of the way as a prelude to what for me was the most exciting part of the evening.

After all the grapes had been mashed and the empty boxes stacked, it was time for us to remove our shoes, socks, and pants and slip into the cool, dark moisture for the traditional grape stomping. This was done, of course, to break up the skins, but I couldn't have cared less why it was necessary. For me it was a sensual experience unlike any other, feeling the grape residue gushing between my toes and watching as the new wine turned my legs the rich, deep color of Cabernet Sauvignon.

While this "man's work" was being accomplished, the "woman's work" was progressing in the kitchen. The heady fragrance of the crushed grapes, mingled with the savory aromas of dinner wafting from the house, caused our feet to move in step with our growing appetites. The traditional main course for our wine-making dinner was gnocchi, a small, dumplinglike pasta that would be cooked to perfection and topped with a wonderful sauce that had been simmering for hours.

Like Christmas Eve, this particular night was unique in many ways. Throughout the rest of the year, we routinely sat down to dinner by 5:30 each evening. But for this occasion dinner was never served until the wine making was finished, sometimes as late as 10 P.M. By then, we were all purple from grape juice, exhausted, and famished.

No matter how tired and hungry we were, however, Papa always prefaced the dinner with a dissertation on "the wine experience." This ceremony called for his finest wines, which had been aging in his modest but efficient wine cellar. Drinking wine, he would remind us, was a highly respected activity, not to be taken lightly. The nectar of the grape had brought joy to human beings long before recorded history.

"Wine is a delight and a challenge and is never meant to be drunk quickly. It's to be savored and sipped slowly," he'd tell us. "All the senses are awakened when you drink wine. You drink with your eyes, your tongue, your throat, your nose. Notice the colors the wine makes in the glass—all the way from dark purple, like a bishop's robe, to the golden amber of an aspen leaf."

He would hold up the glass to the light as if we were about to share a sacrament, then swirl the wine around in his glass, guiding us through the whole ritual, from the first sip to the final, all-important swallow.

"Alla salute!"

Mama always protested (though not too strongly) that he would make drunkards of us all, but Papa shrugged off her comments, saying, "If children are taught to appreciate, they will never abuse." Finally, after the lesson, dinner commenced. I could not have imagined at the time that Papa's lessons would one day richly reward me.

The payoff came many years later when I was in New York with several college friends who had invited me to visit them. They were aware that my meager salary as an elementary schoolteacher would be stretched to the limit by the trip, so they had pooled resources to treat me to a week of theater, opera, and ballet as a birthday celebration.

A party was arranged at a particularly elegant restaurant, long since closed, called the Forum of the Twelve Caesars. It was not a restaurant for eating, but for *dining*. It had heavily polished wood tables, pewter place settings, and oversized leather-upholstered chairs. The maître d' and waiters wore togalike outfits. There were two wine stewards in full Roman regalia, each with a silver chain and cup suspended from his neck. Imposing portraits of the twelve Caesars oversaw our every move. Although we were greeted warmly upon entering this opulent environment, the setting was intimidating. I would have been much more comfortable in a mom-and-pop restaurant on Bleecker Street.

My friends had agreed that a special wine was in order on this auspicious evening. The wine steward was duly impressed with the selection (the price of one bottle commanded *everyone's* attention). With a dramatic motion, he cut the foil capsule from the top of the bottle, then expertly popped the cork and handed it to me. I was the designated taster. All at once, even from three thousand miles away, Papa came to my aid. "Don't worry. Just remember what I taught you, *Felice*," I could almost hear him saying. "Check the cork to see if the bottle has been properly stored. Touch the cork with your finger and put it briefly to your nose. If it's damp and seems right, nod to the steward so he can pour the wine."

Papa's knowledge guided me precisely through the process: Swirl the wine around in the glass without spilling it. Good. Now take a moment to examine the color in the light. Put your nose close to the glass and check the aroma. Good. Now put a very small amount in your mouth. Swish it about. Breathe. Now, swallow. (Thanks, Papa!)

Instantly I realized that something was wrong with this wine. Though I didn't have the exact words to describe it, it seemed acidic, unpleasant, harsh, more like the dark vinegar Mama always splashed on salads.

All eyes were on me. The wine steward seemed to grow visibly taller, towering over me and glaring like one of the Caesars on the wall. I paused and tasted again, with mounting anxiety. What should I do? I had no past experience with this particular wine to call upon. Perhaps rare old vintage wines were supposed to taste like this. Perhaps I should just be silent, accept the wine, and avoid possible embarrassment. At that moment of indecision, the voice of Papa suddenly resounded in my ears.

"*Felice!*" he spoke sternly. "Have I taught you nothing? Your friends are spending a lot of money to buy you a fine wine for your birthday. Do you want to waste their money? The responsibility is yours. You're the taster. Now speak up!"

I surveyed my friends, then looked at the steward, took a deep breath, and heard myself say, rather meekly, "I'm sorry, but I think this wine is past its prime. It's very high in acidity, like vinegar. I think it's spoiled." I heard muted gasps from those around the table.

The wine steward raised an eyebrow and looked at me with disbelief. "The Forum of the Twelve Caesars has one of the finest wine cellars in the world. I hardly think—" He caught himself and did not continue.

At this point my dear friends had all but disappeared into their plush leather chairs. Only Papa, still mystically at my side, maintained his composure.

"Nevertheless," Papa whispered.

"Nevertheless," I echoed.

"Would you mind if I taste it, sir?" the steward questioned, somewhat condescendingly.

"Not at all," I told him.

With exaggerated ceremony, he raised his cup and poured a splash of the wine into it. He carefully brought it to his nose, then to his lips.

Silence. Hesitation. Retaste. Agitation. Confusion.

"Oh, my dear sir," he muttered. "You're right, sir. I can't imagine, sir. This has never happened before. I'm so sorry." His expression softened. "I assure you that the Forum of the Twelve Caesars will be most pleased to offer you all the complimentary wine you care to drink with your dinner."

Triumph!

I really can't recall much about the dinner itself, or how the evening ended. I was too elated and eager to call Papa in Los Angeles before too late an hour. With the sound of success ringing in my voice, I told Papa the entire story. I remember his answer to this day. "*Bravo, Felice,*" he said, obviously pleased. "What did they take you for? Besides," he added, "that wine steward was a fraud. If he had been a true oenophile, he never would have questioned your taste. That's what you get for going to a cheap restaurant!"

PAPA,

the Patriot

THE UNITED STATES OF AMERICA

ORIGINAL
TO BE GIVEN TO
THE PERSON NATURALIZED

No. 4797874

CERTIFICATE OF NATURALIZATION

Petition No. 72175

Personal description of holder as of date of naturalization. Age 53 years; sex Male color White
complexion Dark color of eyes Brown color of hair Black height 5 feet 9 inches
weight 170 pounds; visible distinctive marks None
Marital status Married former nationality Italian
I certify that the description above given is true and that the photograph affixed hereto is a likeness of me.

(Complete and true signature of holder)

(SECURELY AND PERMANENTLY

EDGE OF THE PHOTOGRAPH

Seal

UNITED STATES OF AMERICA
SOUTHERN DIST. OF CALIFORNIA } ss:

Be it known, that ROCCO BARTOLOMEO BUSCAGLIA
then residing at 5111 Fairmount St., Los Angeles, Calif.,
having petitioned to be admitted a citizen of the United States of America, and at
a term of the District Court of The United States held pursuant to law at
Los Angeles on JUN 14 1940 19
the court having found that the petitioner intends to reside permanently in the
United States, had in all respects complied with the Naturalization Laws of the
States in such case applicable, and was entitled to be so admitted, the co
ordered that the petitioner be admitted as a citizen of the United St
In testimony whereof the seal of the court is hereunto
day of June in the year of our
forty and of our
and sixty-fourth.

Fathering may be good for men as well as for children.

—ROSS D. PARKE

Papa was always first in line at the polling place. He never missed an election. Nothing short of a catastrophe could keep him away. When the doors opened at 7 A.M., there he was, waiting to be the first to enter. For a time, being first to vote became a contest between Papa and his good friend Arni Goldstein, a Jewish immigrant from Poland. It seemed to represent something very special to both of them. To my knowledge it was always a friendly sort of competition, as each one attempted to arrive earlier than the other. But Arni finally gave up.

When Papa first came to the United States, his destination was Gallup, New Mexico, where there was work to be had in the mines. He had been preceded by his brother and assured of a job. Like so many immigrants bound for America at the turn of the century, my father was induced to leave his homeland for a well-paying, steady job. Dreams of a better life took form even in remote villages such as Papa's, as stories of golden opportunities were spread. In Papa's case, he was parted from his new wife and one-year-old child, leaving behind the only way of life he had ever known. But it seemed to him worth the separation if it meant an escape from a vicious cycle of poverty and exploitation. A hope for a better life beckoned half a world away.

The plan was that Papa would go to America and work hard until he had accumulated enough money to send for his family. His long-term plan was to amass a small fortune, buy a home, educate his children, then return to his small village to live out his years in security and dignity. That was the scenario for many immigrants, but it did not quite work out that way, either for Papa or for most others.

The majority of immigrants never went back again. The United States became their permanent home. Their dreams eventually faded into nostalgia for their homeland, expressed plaintively on cold winter nights and during long, hot summers. They lived out their days in a love-hate relationship with the Old World and the New.

So it was with Papa.

The stark reality of the damp, dark mines of New Mexico hardly proved the opportunity Papa had envisioned. It wasn't long before he and his brother borrowed some money and set off. They arrived in the Plaza de Nuestra Señora de Los Angeles with sixty-seven cents between them, unable to speak English, and friendless. Papa always told us the story, astounding but true, of how they wandered, lost, near the train station, trying to figure out their next move. Then came a miracle! They encountered a man from their Italian village.

To meet someone at such a time, in such a place, from a town with a population of fewer than two hundred inhabitants, had to be something more than coincidence. Their friend took them home, fed them, and assured them that he'd take care of them until they found jobs.

The next day they found positions as dishwashers in a small restaurant on North Broadway in downtown Los Angeles. Soon Papa was promoted to waiter and finally became the maître d'.

Mama arrived in Los Angeles a year later, a frightened young woman with a small child in her arms. She had to be detained on Ellis Island until her son got over the measles. When she was finally allowed to enter the country, she was no longer sure she would be met by Papa. She feared that he had given up. But Papa met every train from New York for the long weeks that it took for Mama to finally descend into his arms on the train platform in Los Angeles.

I have never ceased to be overwhelmed by the courage of my parents. They were so young when they came to America, so naive, never having been out of their rural village, speaking not a word of English, and with only a pittance in their pockets.

Things began to reverse themselves after Mama's arrival. She took over the management of their modest, two-room house, her first real home. She took in washing and ironing and, like Papa, worked day and night. At times it must have seemed to them that they were once again trapped in their old life style. What kept them going was the inner knowledge that they were working together for a better life and, for the first time, a decent wage.

It wasn't long before there were more children, a larger home, and finally, a newfound feeling of security. They told us often that in those early years they all but lost their youth in the struggle to survive. They missed knowing what it was to be young.

I was about sixteen when Papa announced that he was going to apply for American citizenship. What had delayed this decision for so many years was the English fluency requirement that a citizen had to fulfill. Having gotten by for years with imperfect English, he nonetheless decided to formally upgrade his language skills. He joined a night class at the local elementary school and prepared in earnest to take the naturalization exam.

It was wonderful that Papa, who had loved learning and been denied an education when he was young, could, in middle age, return to the classroom. His excitement and pleasure were obvious. Immediately he bought a large notebook, writing paper, and a dictionary. He picked his clothes for the first night of school with great care. He even got a haircut for the occasion.

On that important evening he rushed through dinner—which was unheard of—put on a suit and tie, picked up his notebook, kissed Mama good-bye as if he were setting off on a six-week cruise, and left!

Papa loved being a student. Every evening after dinner he would gather his books and papers and settle in to do his homework. We thought it was hilarious, but of course we never dared tell Papa that. He would often study a blue pamphlet issued by the Immigration and Naturalization Service titled "What Every U.S. Citizen Should Know."

Papa was far more diligent than his children, and he was continually appalled at how little we knew about our country. "What do they teach you in school?" he'd ask angrily. He'd warn us, "You should know your rights so no one can take them away from you."

It wasn't long before Papa could recite the Pledge of Allegiance and the Preamble to the Constitution. He memorized the Bill of Rights and, much to our amazement, learned the names, in order, of the first thirty presidents of the United States. He knew all the states and their capitals. He could tell you the most important signers of the Declaration of Independence as well as endless lists of historic dates, names, and places. He insisted that we quiz him in every spare moment, rattling off the answers before we could finish the questions.

Who discovered America? "Christoforo Columbus, in 1492."

Who were the first inhabitants of America? "Da Indianos."

Who were the Pilgrims? "Some nice-a people who came, like me and Mama, to America on a boat, da *Mayflower*, in 1620."

His favorite question was, What is a democracy? I think he liked the rhythm of the answer as much as he did the idea. "A government of da people, by da people, for da people."

He would use his newfound knowledge to enrich casual conversations with family and friends. "Don't forget," he'd remind them, "dis is a government of da, by da, and for da people."

Papa loved his teacher and was very popular in his citizenship class. He was continually winning awards of merit: He was given a certificate for being the only member of his class who could recite the Gettysburg Address without a single error. He received a medal—honorable mention—for his short speech titled "Why I Came to America."

At last, Papa was ready to take his final exams. This was, as I still remember, a tense time in our household. For days prior to his having to appear at the Los Angeles Federal Building for his exam, we all walked on eggs. Mama, in her infinite wisdom, advised us to stay away from home as much as possible. When we *were* at home, she suggested we become invisible. We all looked to Papa's eyes to tell us whether it was a time for levity or for silence.

It was with a great sense of relief that we watched Papa leave the house, with his required two witnesses at his side, to take the exam. No sooner had he left than Mama started praying: rosaries to Our Blessed Mother, special vows to Our Blessed Father, flowers and candles to a myriad of saints.

"You don't have to pray, Mama," we assured her. "Papa knows everything. He knows more than the judge." We wouldn't allow ourselves even to imagine what life would be like if Papa failed to pass.

Happily, when he returned a few hours later, his face shone with the unmistakable light of success. I can still picture him striding triumphantly up the walkway in what was undoubtedly one of his proudest moments.

Papa attributed his success to his having studied long and hard. Mama knew better. Though she never dared mention it to Papa, she was convinced that God had been responsible. Be that as it may, Papa's victory was made all the sweeter because the examiner had singled him out for special recognition. He had commented on Papa's fine preparation and had suggested that he was going to make an outstanding citizen.

Even with this honor, Papa was disappointed that he had not been asked enough questions. After all his studying, anxiety, and worry, only three things were asked of him: What is the highest court in the land? Who was the third president of the United States? What is a democracy? His preface to each of his responses, according to witnesses, was, "That's a easy one."

To celebrate his success, Papa took everyone out to dinner. This was seldom done in our family. But on this special occasion he gathered up his teacher, his best friend from class, Mr. Goldstein, and the whole family for a graduation party of sorts. And in keeping with his new status, I remember Papa discussing with Mr. Goldstein how they would vote in the next election.

The swearing-in ceremony was all that was left to make Papa, at last, a real citizen. With hundreds of others, he was required to take the oath of allegiance. We all dressed in our Sunday-go-to-church outfits, squeezed into our dilapidated car, and drove to the courthouse downtown, where the final ceremony was scheduled.

When we entered, the citizens-to-be and their families were separated. Papa was soon lost in a crowd of people whose cultural diversity seemed less apparent in the light of their shared accomplishment. I remember very little about the ceremony itself except for the moment when Papa spotted us in a sea of spectators and waved happily.

Later, after we all hugged him with loving congratulations, he said, "You see. I'm an American now." He paused for a moment and became very pensive. Then he added, "Of Italian descent!" And that was true of Papa forever.

PAPA,

the Environmentalist

To show a child what has once delighted you,
to find the child's delight added to your own,
so that there is now a double delight seen in the
glow of trust and affection. This is happiness.

—J. B. PRIESTLEY

Natural beauty of any sort always brings Papa to mind. He was continually teaching me to "look," "see," "appreciate," "enhance." Not that Papa was a consciously active environmentalist; he simply had a deep love for beautiful things. It seemed natural that he wanted to instill in his children this reverence for beauty and the spirit of the earth. He considered the world a perfect place—God's perfect gift to us—and we therefore had a responsibility to keep it that way. He was a daily model of this in our home and its surrounding gardens.

I have no difficulty recalling in detail the house in which I was born. It was a simple wooden structure, referred to by the lofty title of Craftsman House. It was painted pink (yes, pink) with a light blue border and had a pale yellow picket fence around it. To say the least, the house made a statement. The front gate opened onto a concrete walk leading to a veranda, which served as the entranceway to the living room.

The front yard was a profusion of flowers in wooden planters and within brick borders that broke the symmetry of the lawn. A plaster-of-Paris fawn, feeding with its head lowered, bent over the grass. Though we hated it, it remained Papa's pride. Planters completely surrounded the house, giving the impression that it was floating on a flower bed. Depending on the time of the year, there were hyacinths, ranunculuses, delphiniums, and poinsettias, names that sounded as exquisite to me as the flowers themselves.

Passersby would often stop to congratulate Papa on the beauty his efforts brought to the neighborhood. Papa would modestly reply that it was not his but God's work that was responsible. He would inevitably follow this announcement by presenting them with one of "God's flowers" to take along with them to brighten their day.

My presence was required during precious weekends to help Papa fight the endless battle of the bugs. Wielding shears, Papa clipped, cut, tied, trimmed, trained, and fertilized, while I tidied and watered after him. Our work was always accompanied by flowery lectures.

While I would much rather have been in the street playing baseball with my friends, Papa would wax poetic about the spirit of the earth. He would explain the whole process of growth as a miracle, from the planting of a seed in the dark, damp soil, to the sprouting of the flower. I would remind him that he'd told me that story only the week before, but this would not deter him. "It's God's miracle," he'd continue. "Each seed will become its own flower. There is never any mistake. A sweet pea will grow to become a sweet pea. This one will become an aster. Isn't that amazing?"

I couldn't help wondering if Papa was slightly retarded to believe that such an obvious fact was a miracle. Even in my childish ignorance I knew that an iris seed would not become an aster. Of course, it never occurred to me to consider why this was a fact of nature. Experience had taught me to humor Papa in such things, lest he decide to expound further and keep me longer from the baseball game.

Our backyard was Papa's principal domain. He had developed a fantasy garden from a plot of land where wind, waterlogged soil, and insects gave battle but never gained the upper hand. These forces had no chance when pitted against Papa's patience and loving skills as a nurturer.

Year after year, his success was apparent, as neat rows of lettuce, radishes, onions, carrots, cabbage, potatoes, and of course, garlic, began to appear. The poles he erected to interconnect the beans and the tomato plants were always strained to the breaking point. And the garden never lacked for tender leaves of Swiss chard, which Mama prepared in countless ways, all delicious. But the bumper crop each year was the zucchini. Papa had a special way with zucchini.

Among all this plenty there were fruit trees—a loquat, an orange, a peach, a pear, and a fig.

There was an herb garden that Papa had planted especially for Mama, conveniently near the kitchen. Before each meal one could find her bent over this aromatic plot, picking a bit of this and that, a potpourri to enhance the coming feast. Food in our home was never bland.

There were gorgeous flowers in Papa's garden, too. A special plot was used solely by Mama, who cut and placed flowers before the statue of Jesus she kept on her dresser. These blossoms were also carried by the armful to decorate the graves of the family and friends who had died.

Papa and I had a Saturday-morning ritual that was never broken. We would rise early, have breakfast, then go out into the garden for our weekly check. This we did to keep track of and gloat over our handiwork. "Just look," Papa would say again and again while he peeled back a dying leaf to expose, for my benefit, signs of new growth hiding under it. He'd lift a section of a bush or a branch to reveal an exotic fruit or flower that otherwise had been out of my sight. He'd unearth a green plant to show me how the seed we had planted had become a vegetable, ripe for eating. He'd peel a loquat, a peach, or a pear for us to savor together, like a mysterious ritual, a secret to be shared only between us.

"Always have a place to grow things," he advised me. "People who don't have experience with growing things don't really ever understand what life is all about." Every Saturday I heard him repeat an old Italian proverb: "The man who helps things to grow is never too far from the smile of God."

Papa tended his garden with the same loving concentration usually reserved for a mother nurturing her child. He would center in on a diseased plant, an aphid, or a snail with the focus of an artist. His garden was his meditation place, his cathedral. When Papa was in his temple, there was no communicating with him. There was no choice but to wait until he returned to earth.

For me, harvesting was always the most fun—getting the ladders in place and scrambling up into the branches of the trees to pick the fruit, pulling the vegetables out of the ground, gathering the tomatoes and zucchini, and picking string beans. Buckets of water were always in place to wash off the fresh-smelling soil. Each piece of fruit or vegetable was washed and shaken and dried before it was dropped into Mama's apron. Sometimes, I'd pop a morsel of our harvest into my mouth and experience the unique taste of a crunchy, fresh carrot or the crispness of a string bean eaten raw, fully ripened on the vine.

As Papa grew older and seemed to shrink slightly under the weight of age, so did his garden. Fewer and fewer plots were planted each year. But he always had a garden—even until the last weeks of his life. When Papa sold the family home after Mama died, the new owners had no interest in gardening and allowed his garden to die, strangled by weeds or suffocated under newly laid concrete.

Papa could never bear to go back again. I think the house mattered less to him than the garden. A house, he reasoned, is a dead thing, really living only in the memories of those who are alive in it. The garden is a different matter. The earth is always vital and alive.

Even left abandoned, fruit trees still attempt to bear, bulbs continue to fight the hardening soil. So to him, abandoning a plot of land was a form of unforgivable devastation against which he struggled all his life.

Papa's love for the environment continued almost to the day of his death. During his last days in the hospital, the ward nurses told me of having entered his room to find him missing. They searched frantically and finally discovered him outside in his robe, watering a small garden that was visible from his window. "No one is taking care of these plants, and they're about to die," he explained to the nurses. "It's such a pity when all they need to live is just a little water."

To this day I cannot see a bright daffodil, a proud gladiola, or a smooth eggplant without thinking of Papa. Like his plants and trees, I grew up as a part of his garden. That experience has left me with a reverence for nature and beauty that I'll never lose. Papa taught me a deep respect for nurturing and a sense of responsibility for keeping the world, as well as my own backyard, a growing place, a tribute to the miracle of life.

PAPA,

the Nurturer

The last time my dad and I were together I was in Nashville, where he and Mom lived. The two of us were in the car. He was driving, in his cowboy hat and coat. We were enjoying the moment. Then I looked at him chewing on his pipe, and was suddenly deeply moved. I had to say what was in my heart. It took a lot of nerve for me to speak up because he was so reserved.

I said, "I just want to thank you for being my father. I think you're the greatest man I ever met and I love you."

He smiled slowly before he said, "Yes, son, that's very nice."

"Dad, I'd like to hear you say it, too."

"What?"

"Do you like me?"

"Well, I love you."

"Then let me hear it." And he did. Three weeks later he was gone.

—JOHN RITTER

I wonder why it seems so difficult to tell our fathers that we love them?

One assignment I never failed to give as part of my Love Class at the University of Southern California always caused a stir. I suggested that all the students, on their next visit home, embrace their fathers and verbally express their love for them. "We can't do that," most of the students would exclaim. "He'd die if I hugged him! Anyway, my dad knows that I love him. I don't have to say it to him."

"Then it should be easy to do the assignment, so go do it!" was my response.

Oddly, most of these same individuals never seemed to have a problem hugging their mothers.

It was always interesting when they had completed the task. Inevitably, when they reported the results to the class, they would be astonished at what a positive and poignant experience it had been.

"I couldn't believe it. My dad cried."

"It was strange; my father thanked me for the hug."

The common experience was that most fathers were overwhelmed by the experience, as well as very responsive to it.

Outward expression of affection was never a problem in our home. It became an issue only when we *failed* to express it. We grew up touching, hugging, and kissing each other, and have continued to express affection for each other in this way to this day. One of Papa's favorite expressions was, "It costs nothing to be nice. It costs nothing to love." Mama's and Papa's arms were always ready to open wide.

I could never understand why such a common show of affection was not the norm in other families. My friends, especially as I grew older, made fun of me, calling me a baby and snickering that I still kissed my father. Though they were always quick to disdain any show of affection or expression of tenderness, it was apparent to me that they were intrigued by it, even a bit envious. They gradually came to accept this behavior in the same way they did our other "eccentricities"—the odd food we ate, the strange accent we had, and the animated way we talked to each other.

As much as I wanted to conform to my peer group (especially in adolescence), it never occurred to me to give up something as nice as hugs.

One place we could always be assured of hugs was on Papa's lap. It was a royal area where we could find security and peace to be found nowhere else. I always associate a wonderfully pleasant scent of earth and herbs with sitting on Papa's lap. When I settled in, I could stay for hours. I dared not move for fear that I might cause Papa some discomfort and be asked to leave. At times he'd brush my hair with his hand or lean over and kiss my head. There, in Papa's lap, I was special, and things were always right. I always knew his lap would be there—mine, when I needed it.

Though Papa was often accused of being too soft, no one ever questioned his masculinity. Papa was "the boss" at our house, or at least that was the projected impression. He always called the shots, but deference to Mama's wishes was implicit in the order of things. When there was a disagreement, Mama knew when to back off. She'd say, "What good is it to win an argument and lose a good man?"

So it appeared that Papa always got his way. In the last analysis, it wasn't true, but if we ever dared to suggest this, Mama would deny it vehemently, accuse us of impertinence, and threaten us with violence. Mama had her own definition of diplomacy.

One of the special privileges I had as a child was to be invited by Papa to join him on a visit to a neighbor, or to go with him to early mass on Sunday morning. Of course, it required special clothes for the occasion. Since Papa always wore a coat and tie for such outings, I also had to wear, at the very least, a clean, starched shirt, long pants, and shined shoes. Papa told me time and again that he wanted to be proud of me, and I was always anxious not to disappoint him.

He'd take my hand firmly in his and we would be off: he so tall, straight, and dignified at my side, and I, with my short legs, running to keep up with him, two steps to his one, striving to get into his rhythm. I was amazed that this handsome man I looked up to was my father.

One visit I always looked forward to was with the family who lived on the corner. They had a large house with an ivy-covered veranda. There I'd sit for an afternoon with Papa and his friends. I would listen to them for hours as they recalled memories of their beloved Italia.

They told such wonderful stories of the "old country," an enchanting, faraway place about which I never tired of hearing. They would end by laughing boisterously or, often, in silent tears. The nostalgia grew with each sip of homemade wine. I was given a cold drink and expected to be silent unless spoken to. In spite of that, I was content to be there. It was as if I were being initiated into my father's secret world, long since behind him but no less important or real, even with the passage of time.

I was happy to suffer anything to share these private times with Papa. I sometimes got up at dawn to go with him to mass and sit quietly in a pew for hours, not moving (or complaining) until he was ready to take me by the hand and leave.

Papa was not always gentle and tolerant. He was a very firm disciplinarian when the situation warranted it. He had a temper that was often fierce and flaring. His idea of punishment was radically different from Mama's. If we got out of line and Mama felt that a lesson needed to be taught, it was offered on the spot, no matter where or when. It would usually be preceded by the familiar expression "*Ti spacco la faccia,*" which, freely translated, describes the lesson excellently: "I'll smash your face." Though Mama's hand was no less punishing than Papa's, there was a difference. Once done, it was over. She wiped our tears, explained what we had to learn from the experience, and that was that.

Papa had a different style with which we were only too well acquainted. First we were warned with what we came to call the evil eye, a look that said it all. His eyes would burn and pierce us with meaning. If we were wise enough to heed the warning, it usually ended there. If we ignored the cue, or were stupid enough to defy it, we could expect no mercy.

If consistency is the food of love, we were well fed. Papa never forgot. A beating from Papa was no fun. His anger came in waves and seemed to last forever. We learned to expect a respite between spankings, waiting an hour for the inevitable second helping. I must admit that it was easy to hate Papa at these times. But this is the way we learned what, for Papa, was right and wrong. In looking back, I can't say that I profited from the physically punitive lessons, but I can say that Papa was consistent and never so hypocritical as to tell me that it hurt him more than it did me.

Papa grew more mellow with age until it became difficult to see him as the same man I'd known in my youth. In fact, at the time of publication of *Love*, wherein I first described Papa as tender, loving, and warm, my brother, who was much older than I and had known our father in his younger days, told me, "The father you describe was certainly not mine."

I resented his observation at first, then it dawned on me that Papa indeed had changed over the years. Age had softened him. The man my brother knew as a father was not the same one I'd known. People change—even fathers.

Papa's nurturing extended to every conceivable animal. I can't remember a time when we didn't have a dog, a couple of cats, birds, goldfish, rabbits, chickens, and now and then a turtle. They were all shown the same attention and loving care that Papa shared with his family. Under his protection the rabbits multiplied even more rapidly than usual, the chickens kept us and our neighbors supplied with fresh eggs, the birds kept singing from morning until night.

Papa had a nurturing attitude about food as well. Sunday was his day in the kitchen, and Mama's day to sleep late and go to high mass at her leisure. Though we dared not say so, I think we all agreed that our most memorable meals came on Sunday. It's not that Papa was a better cook than Mama, it was just that he took greater care and was more inventive. He had only one rule: Mama had to stay out of the kitchen. Since he was invading her domain, he knew that she would not be easily satisfied and, of course, he was right. No matter how spectacular were the dishes he served, Mama was always able to find fault with them.

"This would be perfect if it had just a dash more

salt." "This needs a little more cooking." "You could have put in a pinch more oregano." This became some sort of game between them, and we would wince with each criticism, anticipating the time when Papa would explode and never again return to the kitchen. It never happened.

Years later, when there were only the two of them in the house, Mama gave up cooking altogether. She announced one day that she had cooked enough for a lifetime. If Papa wanted to eat, he could take over the kitchen or, better yet, they could go out. Papa, frugal as always, became the chef. He took on his new role with the same vigor and pride with which he did all things.

Though Mama seldom praised Papa's cooking, she had her own way of showing her appreciation. She'd take second helpings. Of course, she always had a good sound reason for doing so. "I'd better take a little more of that," she'd say. "We don't want to waste it. People are starving all over the world." Or "There's not enough left in that dish to feed a pigeon. I'll just clean it up." Papa would beam with pride.

Papa has been dead for years, but my hallways still resound with his footsteps, his laugh, and the lilt of his speech. His special glow emerges from memories of secret places and often causes me to pause and picture him as he was.

I can still remember the last time Papa and I shared our love. We were walking on the sand near the ocean at Waikiki. He looked old and tired, and his brisk walk was by now a slow, pained gait. I had an uncontrollable urge to stop right there and take him into my arms and hug him. But Papa, always the nurturer, spared me the trouble. He stopped and reached out to me, took me into his arms, and spoke the very thoughts I wanted to express. "Don't be sad," he said in Italian. "We've had a nice life together."

PAPA,

the Last Days

When Dad died I went through a heavy mourning period, when I felt, "Now he won't know about me." But I've discovered that in some ways he's still there. I can go to the beach and talk to myself and get feedback. I don't mean anything otherworldly. It's just that I can still look to the example my father set and get the sustenance I need.

—TYNE DALY

Papa was eighty-eight when he died. He outlived Mama by five years. During the difficult and lonely time after Mama died, I never heard him complain. He chose to live alone, in close proximity to my eldest sister, Marge. He took care of himself, did his own housecleaning, shopping, and cooking. And he never stopped caring for his goldfish or his garden.

To the very end he continued to share whatever he had with family and neighbors. He never lost interest in life and learning. He never stopped loving many things with a passion.

Papa's fatal illness was diagnosed a year before he died. This was tragic news, of course, but it afforded us some special time for quiet reminiscences, as well as the opportunity to create new memories. Coming face-to-face with one's mortality has a way of making every moment precious.

Papa took the news of his impending death with the same basic philosophy that had guided him throughout his life: acceptance. "Everybody dies," he told me. "I just have a better idea when it will happen. We don't live forever."

Though Papa shared certain special desires during this time, he seemed most content just to be in his home, surrounded by friends, family, and memories. He did express two wishes, though he insisted it didn't matter whether or not they were realized: He wanted to return to Hawaii, where in the past he had been enthralled by the abundance of things he loved best about the world—flowers, birds, ocean, sand, sunshine, and people.

With a twinkle in his eyes, he also suggested that he'd enjoy a quick trip to Las Vegas. He and Mama had never been able to get over their awe of that city. Both loved to play the nickel slot machines. I think Papa felt sure that one day he'd win the big jackpot.

We were determined that Papa's last wishes be honored. We quickly planned a trip to Hawaii with as many family members as could get away. Though we offered to arrange it, Papa refused to travel first class. He insisted we go as cheaply as possible—the "no frills" fare suited him just fine. Getting there safely was all Papa wanted.

"No frills" meant no food service, and we assumed the flight attendants wouldn't have too much time to spend attending to us passengers who were traveling so cheaply. Papa didn't care about these things. His wisdom convinced him that no matter where one sat on a plane, or how much or little the fare, all the passengers still got there at the same time.

Special-fare passengers had their own section in the rear of the plane. We occupied two rows, with our family members seated together. Knowing that meals would not be provided, we had decided to share potluck and prepare our own. Each of us brought a favorite dish—enough food to fill four shopping bags and feed half the passengers and the crew. Shades of Mama's influence!

Papa laughed that he had come full circle. He had arrived in the United States with a suitcase and a shopping bag and now, after so many years, he still was traveling with the same luggage. It is impossible ever to forget the expressions on the faces of the flight attendants as they handed out their prepared lunches to the other passengers, while we dug into our mysterious bags and produced a meal that could be duplicated only on the finest gourmet tables.

We started our lunch with a delectable antipasto, accompanied by salamis and marinated peppers, one of Papa's favorite dishes. The attendants were amazed to realize that the antipasto was the first course. We were only beginning! From our shopping bags emerged rosemary chicken, fried eggplant and zucchini, crisp Italian bread smothered with garlic. One of the attendants was so impressed that she secretly gave us a complimentary bottle of wine.

Our meal ended with fresh fruit and cheese. We ate all the way to Oahu. Of course, Papa insisted on sharing with his fellow coach passengers. By the time we landed, we still had leftovers enough for three more meals in our hotel.

As we left the plane, the flight attendants informed us that the pungent, heavenly aromas of our lunch had caused several comments from the first-class passengers, who were slightly miffed about those in coach getting more exciting meals than they had.

Our memorable flight only whetted our appetite for the wonderful things to come. Oahu hosted Papa with its ideal weather. We rose early each morning to take long walks on the beach. We ate huge breakfasts, had picnics at Waimea Bay, and bathed among the colorful fish in Kahala.

We spent hours at the bird farm. Papa was never ready for bed. He couldn't seem to get enough of life in Waikiki—the warm breezes, fragrant flowers, beautiful people, and the perfect long-lasting sunsets.

Las Vegas was another matter. It had seemed to us a strange choice of a place for a person who wasn't much of a gambler to want to spend his final days. But there was a crazy side to Papa that Las Vegas seemed to stimulate. He loved the noise, the crowd, the electric excitement. He found the slot machines fascinating and stayed there for hours, sitting with the handle firmly gripped in his hand, waiting for the big one. Though we hoped it would happen, it never did. But at least we made sure that Papa never ran out of nickels.

For all of his life Papa had managed to ignore age. He always looked and acted younger than his years. He saw chronological age as insignificant and certainly not a measure of the quality of his life. But during his final weeks, his physical self began to weigh heavily upon him. Each symptom of his illness, which he had always suffered in silence, took its obvious toll. His vitality waned, his eyes began to lose their sparkle, and his usual ruddy complexion faded.

He began to spend more time sitting in Mama's special chair in his living room, commenting that his chores were taking him so much longer. Even picking his string beans became an arduous task. Though Papa was an avid reader, the books, magazines, and newspapers we brought him began to accumulate, unopened. His joy in eating gave way to picking at his food; soon he enjoyed only cold cereal and fruit.

One evening I was called suddenly with the news that Papa had suffered a stroke and was in the hospital. Though it was not as serious as it at first had seemed, it did drastically affect his eyesight. In fact, when I went to his bedside, he was able to recognize me only by my voice and touch.

"Am I going to be blind?" he asked me that evening.

"I don't know, Papa," I answered honestly.

"Well"—he thought for a while—"it doesn't matter. I've seen so much in my lifetime. I've even lived long enough to see my great-grandchildren. And you know, if the doctor lets me go home again, I can manage even if I can't see at all. I was thinking about it today. I know every inch of my apartment—where I keep the dishes, the pots and pans, the cat's dish, the bird food. I even know exactly how I laid out the garden. I'll get along just fine. I won't bother anyone."

Four days later Papa was gone. It was difficult to imagine a world without him. There were hundreds of people at his funeral—family members and friends, crowds of people we didn't even know. He was buried in the plot next to Mama, which they had prearranged.

To clean out Papa's apartment wasn't an easy task. But the process, in retrospect, did offer some closure. Memories hung in closets, were stored in boxes and drawers and neatly folded in trunks. We found Father's Day ties he had never used, as well as several unopened bottles of cologne we had thrust upon him over the years. And there was a box of family photos, letters, and keepsakes that poignantly revived Papa's past, and our own.

I have long believed that the only immortality we know lies in the love we have left behind in others' memories. So Papa is still very much alive. He's in his kitchen, watering his garden, tending his pets. He's in Italy, Los Angeles, New Mexico, Hawaii, Las Vegas, and with me wherever I go.

There was a strange coincidence the day Papa died. Someone from our old neighborhood, a woman who lived just across the street from our family, called me. She knew nothing of Papa's death—it had happened just the night before her call. "I thought you'd like to know," she told me sadly, "that last night your old family home burned down. It burned right to the ground. I thought your father would like to know. He spent so much time and love on that house."

Realistically, I know that the burning of the house was just a startling coincidence. But in my heart I like to think that the old house, having shared so many years of happiness, so many wonderful years with Papa, decided it was time for it to go, too.

PAPA,

the Legend and the Legacy

The words a father speaks to his children in the privacy of the home are not overheard at the time, but as in whispering galleries, they will be heard at the end and by posterity.

—JEAN PAUL FRIEDRICH RICHTER

I have much to thank Papa for. He helped me to grow up more or less sane, a healthy neurotic who laughs a lot, loves a lot, and isn't afraid to cry or be vulnerable. He showed me that life is an exciting adventure and challenged me to take full advantage of all it has to offer. He hooked me on learning and taught me my responsibility for leaving the world a better place for my having been in it.

I'm aware that my life has not been the greatest success story, but, like Papa, I am far from a failure. The facts of life that Papa modeled for me were simple. He lived by a positive code, the rules of which were uncomplicated and accessible to anyone wanting to live a good life.

Dance, sing, and laugh a lot.

All things are related.

Don't waste time trying to reason with pain, suffering, life, and death.

An animated person animates the world.

Find a quiet place for yourself.

Don't ever betray yourself.

Birth and death are part of a cycle. Neither begins or ends with you.

Stay close to your God.

It's crucial to love.

Idealism is a strength, not a weakness.

People are good if you give them a chance to be.

Discrimination, for any reason, is wrong.

Self-respect is essential for life.

Except in the eyes of God, people are not created

equal, so we are all responsible for those who can't help themselves.

Cruelty is a sign of weakness.

Commitment and caring are the basic ingredients of love.

Love is indestructible and therefore the most powerful human force.

Change is inevitable.

People who think they know it all can be dangerous.

It's true that "everybody gots a father," as the little girl said in the class so many years ago. But there are fathers and there are fathers.

There is always the chance that my deep love for Papa has caused me to be partially blind to his faults. I know he had imperfections and I am not suggesting that he was a candidate for canonization. But I know for certain that he was very much a selfless person, never dishonest or vindictive.

He was proud, sensitive, affectionate. His greatest fault might have been his obsessive need for security and love—if this is a fault. He was compassionate, naturally intelligent, and always concerned about the welfare of others. But no matter what he had or didn't have, was or wasn't, his attitude toward fatherhood made a positive and lasting difference in my life. What else can we ask of another human being?

Thanks, Papa. I'll always love you.